Coloring Your Grief: Coloring to Soothe the Soul and Mend the Heart

Jane V. Bissler, Ph.D., LPCC-S, FT

Sheri L. Goldstrohm, Ph.D.

Phyllis Kosminsky, Ph.D., LCSW, FT

Copyright © 2016 Bissler, Goldstrohm, Kosminsky

All rights reserved.

ISBN: **1523784482**
ISBN-13: **978-1523784486**

To grieving people everywhere, we dedicate this book to you.

CONTENTS

	Acknowledgments	I
1	Introduction	1
2	How to Use the Book	2
3	Approaching the Coloring Book	4
4	Connect to Your Memories	5
5	Open to Your Emotions	15
6	Let Go of All Judgment	27
7	Ongoing Connections	39
8	Reinvest in Yourself	49

ACKNOWLEDGMENTS

The pictures in this coloring book were created by art students from Kent State University in Kent, Ohio. We are grateful to these young artists for helping us bring this project to fruition. Thank you Rachel Bendeum, Kaity Culp, Alexa Sollisch and Allyson Stiffler. Thanks also to art therapist Katie O'Connor from Children's Hospital of Pittsburgh of UPMC for her drawings and comments. To all our contributors, we appreciate your hard work and dedication to this project.

CHAPTER 1
INTRODUCTION

Why a coloring book for grief?

What does a grieving person need? If you or someone you care about has suffered a significant loss, you probably have an idea of what a grieving person needs: time to remember and mourn the one who has died; the comforting presence of family and friends; rest, nourishment, and spiritual connection. People have different ways of healing, but these are a few of the things that many people find helpful. In our work with people who are grieving we have learned that it is often helpful for them to have some balance between quiet time and active time, and between time spent thinking about the person who has died, and time spent thinking about other things. Research on healing from loss suggests that grievers benefit from being able to move back and forth between focusing on the loss and focusing on things other than the loss – their ongoing relationships, work, leisure activities, and so on. This kind of flexible attention is conducive to healing, and it is what this book is designed to help you achieve. You may start with an image that reminds you of your loved one, and then, as you become immersed in the activity of coloring the picture, you may find your thoughts moving in other directions. Or you may simply find that you are not thinking about anything other than how your picture looks and what color to use next.

Another reason for this coloring book has to do with the activity itself. If you haven't colored in a while, you may be surprised to discover how quickly your mind and body begin to calm down and relax when you do. Coloring reduces stress – we know this from experience, and from research on this and other benefits of expressive arts. Maybe it is because it reminds us of childhood. Maybe it is because when we are coloring, we are distracted from adult fears and worries. Maybe, as scientists suggest, it is because activities that involve color and form light up parts of our brains that are different than those that are involved with language and thought. When these creative, imaginative areas of the brain come on line, the result is a kind of vacation for over-used, over-worked parts that are designed to make sense of the world and translate it into words.

Grieving for someone you love can be exhausting, and many of the people we see say that they wish they could just get a bit of a break from their grief, set it aside for an hour or an afternoon. This is what activities like coloring can do. Creative activities promote flexible attention and emotional flow – they free the mind and calm the spirit.

CHAPTER 2
ABOUT THIS BOOK

This coloring book was designed for adults who are experiencing some type of grief or loss. Grief arises as a result of a loss and can be experienced through a wide variety of emotions. Many people struggle to identify and express what they are feeling and experiencing. At times, the experience can feel erratic and may be difficult to process or verbalize. The expressive arts are expressive modalities which can create a pathway to access these challenging emotions. Using an expressive modality can encourage movement to effectively process grief. Expressive modalities, such as coloring, can also provide containment for the grief, a place for it to be held. Coloring can provide a safe way to release tension and more fully encounter what is being experienced, while also helping you make sense of what you are experiencing.

Coloring is not just for kids: it can be beneficial for adults as well. Coloring has been known to have "de-stressing power". For many, the simplicity of the task is found to be soothing. People often report that coloring takes them to a time when life was simple and more carefree. In addition, coloring has been known to have the ability to generate wellness, quietness and also stimulates brain areas related to motor skills, the senses and creativity. Coloring can be a relaxing, meditative, creative, healing experience.

Go slowly, relax, think, feel, experience.

Book Construction:

This coloring book has been created as a self-guided tool to assist in the grief and bereavement process. It was designed to facilitate a non-verbal exploration of the outlined concept areas and to help you recognize and express feelings of grief, discover your own grieving process, and facilitate growth.

Use this book at your own pace. The book is divided into 5 concept areas with specific objectives in each. Move through the book at an appropriate pace for you. Take your time, learn, experience, process, grow.

This book can be used alone or in conjunction with counseling. It is not intended to replace the advice or treatment by physicians, counselors, social workers, psychologists, or other experts. It should be considered an additional resource only. Questions and concerns about mental or physical health should always be discussed with a health care provider.

Please keep in mind that this is your own book. The time and effort you put into completing the pages is for you. This book is something you will be able to keep to help you remember someone special. In the future, you will be able to refer to this work as a glimpse of the journey of your process through grief.

Core Concepts:

This book is divided into 5 sections based on theme-based concepts. The subject matter of the pictures was chosen to encourage meditation and self-reflection.

C - Connect to your memories

O - Open to your emotions

L - Let go of all judgment

O - Ongoing Connections

R - Reinvest in yourself.

CHAPTER 3
APPROACHING THIS COLORING BOOK

These coloring pages are designed as meditation aids and tools for you to be able to reflect deeply on your experience. When you color, relax and focus on the outlined concepts as your hand explores the page. More insights may come to you in a relaxed state.

1. Environment. Find a quiet, private space that will allow you to reflect and experience the journey.

2. Coloring instruments. Use whatever is most comfortable for you. Options include crayons, colored pencils, markers, and gel pens.

3. Pace. Take this book at your own pace. Take your time, relax, and think about the outlined concept while you engage in each coloring activity.

4. Approach. Stay in the lines, deliberately go out of the lines, add things to the picture, leave some key elements uncolored. Do what feels right for you.

5. Use these pages to connect with how you feel. Depending on our mood, you may choose different colors or intensity. Color in whatever shades you are feeling today. Put on some music that sounds like your feelings and color to it.

6. Allow yourself to be open to the experience. You may notice that a color strikes a mood, or a picture triggers a memory. This is an opportunity for your grieving body to speak, be heard, and be externalized.

7. Allow yourself to identify problems, elicit concerns, and express frustrations, hopes, dreams, and/or anxieties.

8. Give each aspect of your grief the attention it deserves and needs. Recall stories and memories.

9. Reflect. Give yourself permission to take a break when needed.

10. Give yourself the opportunity to express yourself without having to put it into words.

11. **This is your book. Do what feels right for you.**

CHAPTER 4
CONNECT TO YOUR MEMORIES

As therapists, we know that connecting to your memories is an important aspect of the grief process. Allow the pictures in this section to remind you of the wonderful times and places you experienced with your loved one.

My sun sets to rise again.
                    Robert Browning

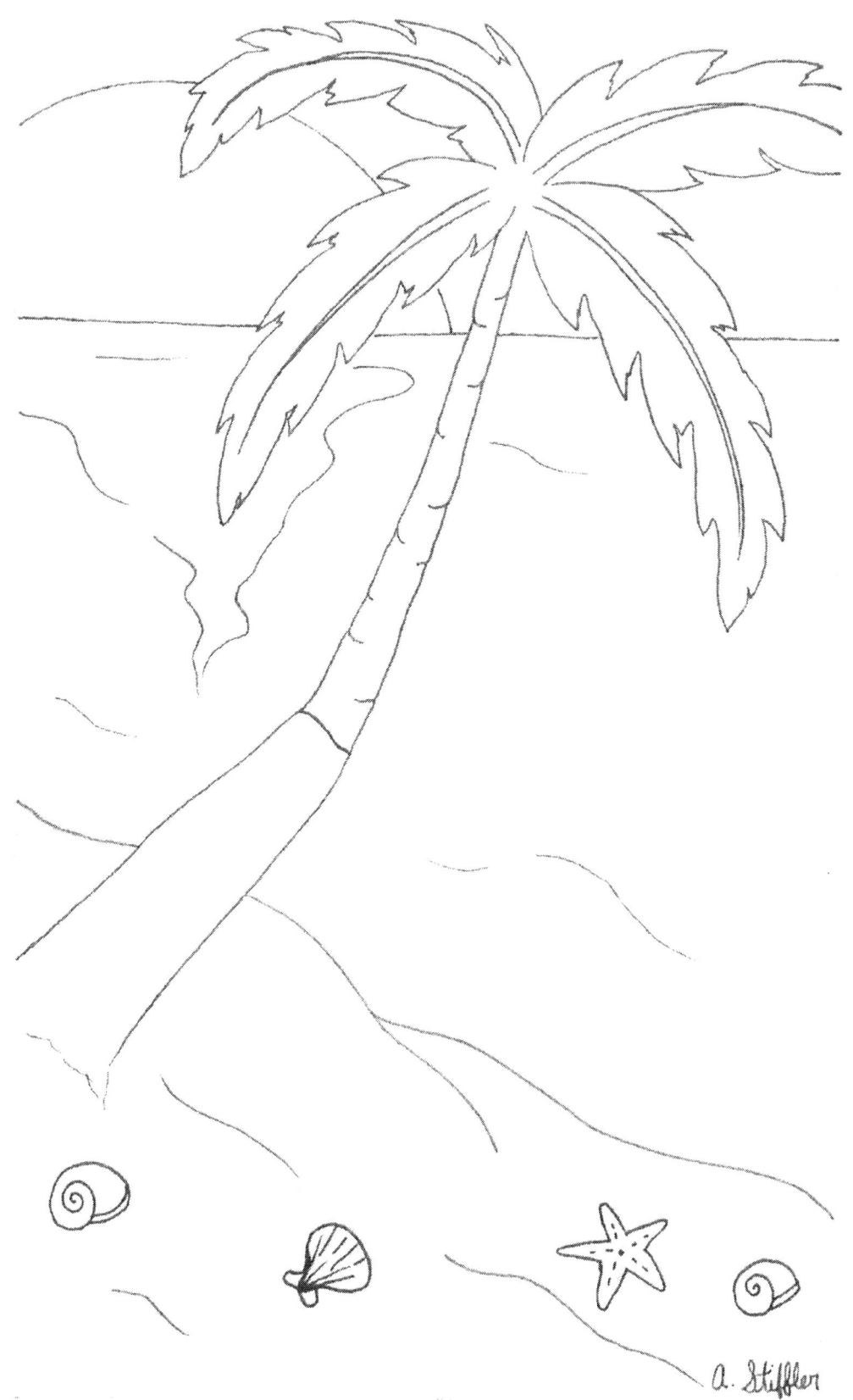

What appears to be a path to some appears to be a barrier to others. When you take the first step, the rest of the pathway may appear.
Author Unknown

Glow brightly, little light, and send my message: "I will love you. Never forget you, always be with you."
Jeri Gingham

The grave is but a covered bridge, leading from light to light, through a brief darkness.
    Henry Wadsworth Longfellow

CHAPTER 5
OPEN TO YOUR EMOTIONS

As we grieve, our emotions can be overwhelming, mysterious, confusing and even scary for some. The pages in this section allow you to be open to whatever you are feeling as the emotional part of your brain begins to reveal itself.

All who have been touched by beauty are touched by sorrow at its passing.
                                        Louis Cordana

I gradually learned to stay connected to my inner world with all the uncomfortable, prickly, and thorny emotions that continually arise.
                                              Philip M. Bark

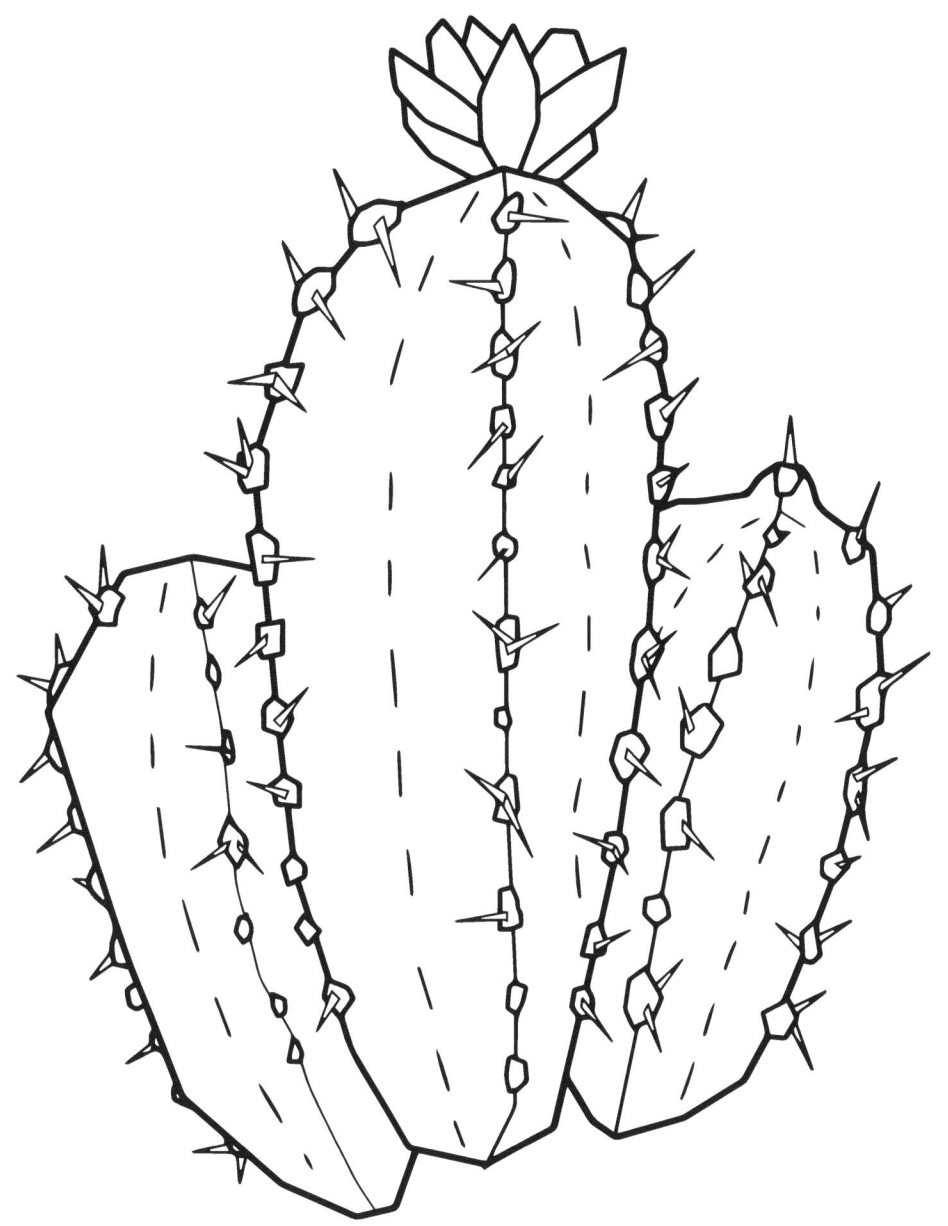

If I should ever leave you whom I love, to go along the silent way, grieve not, nor speak of me with tears, but laugh and talk of me as if I were beside you there.
Isla Paschal Richardson

The walls we build around us to keep sadness out also keep out the joy.

Jim Rohn

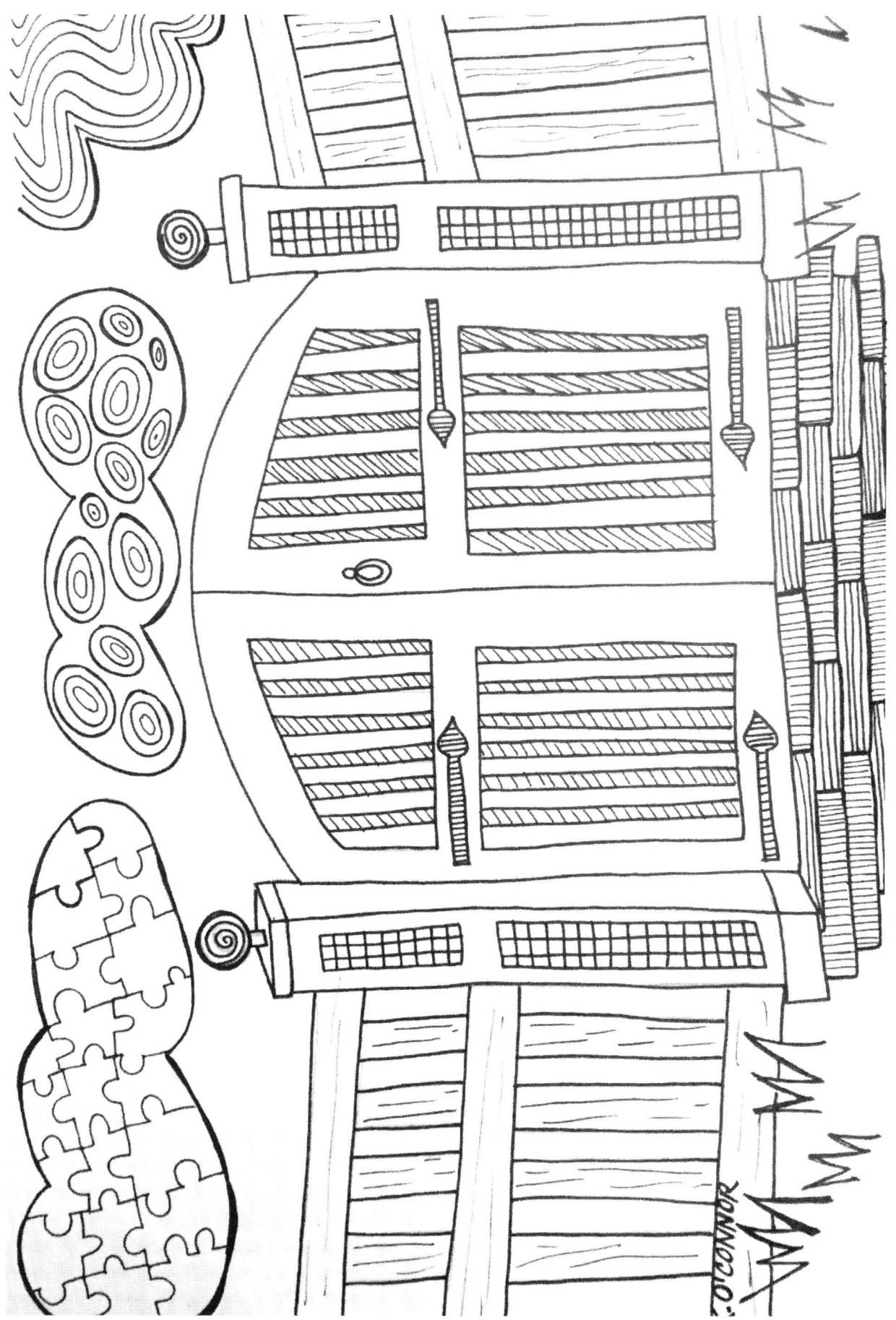

I'm not afraid of storms, for I'm learning how to sail my ship.
Louisa May Alcott

CHAPTER 6
LET GO OF ALL JUDGMENT

Sometimes we have expectations about how we should be dealing with our loss, and we can become critical of ourselves when we do not meet these expectations. As you color the pictures in this section, allow yourself to let go of judgment about your grief and about yourself.

Be kind to yourself.

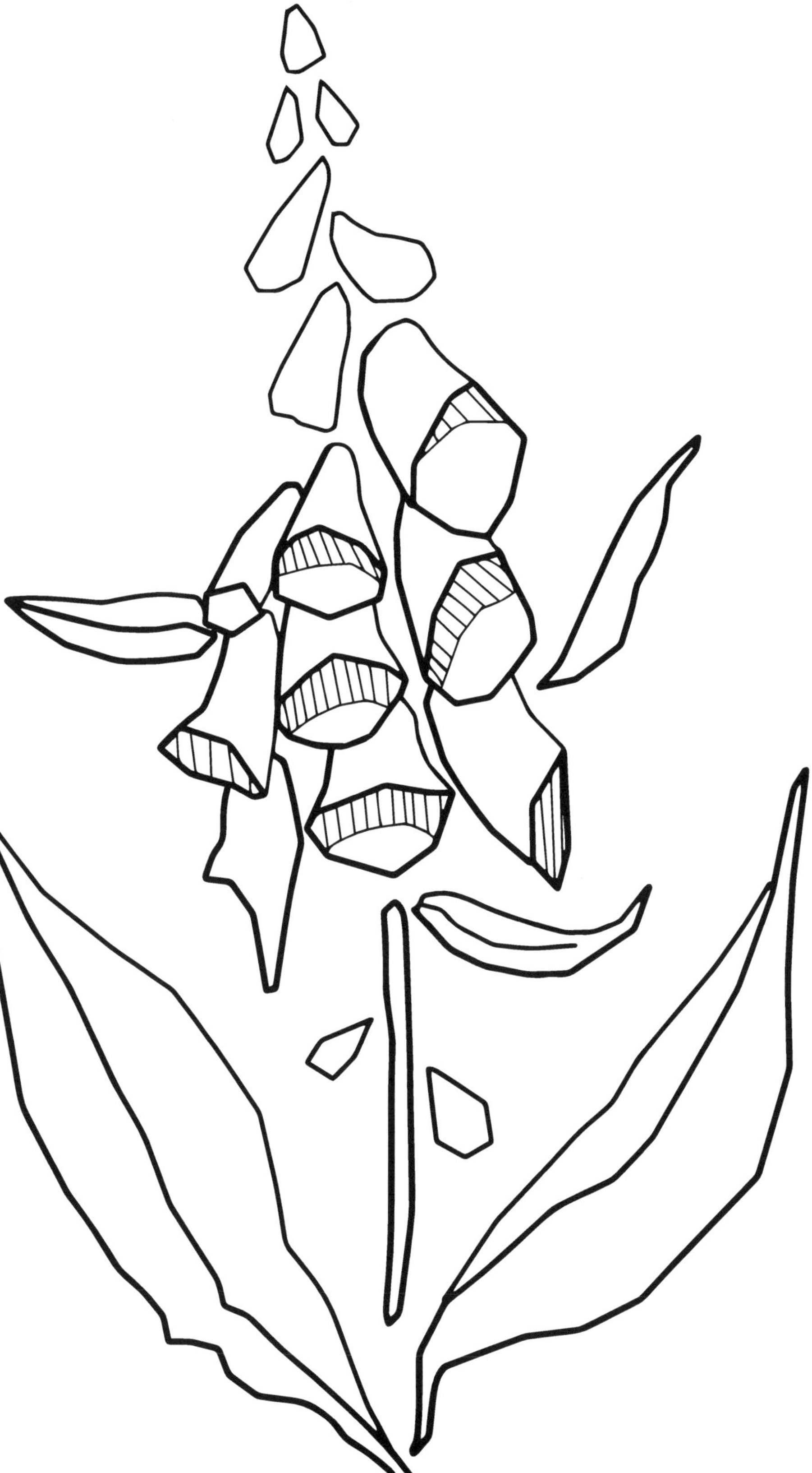

Love is like a balloon, easy to blow up and fun to see grow. But hard to let go and watch fly away.
Author Unknown

I

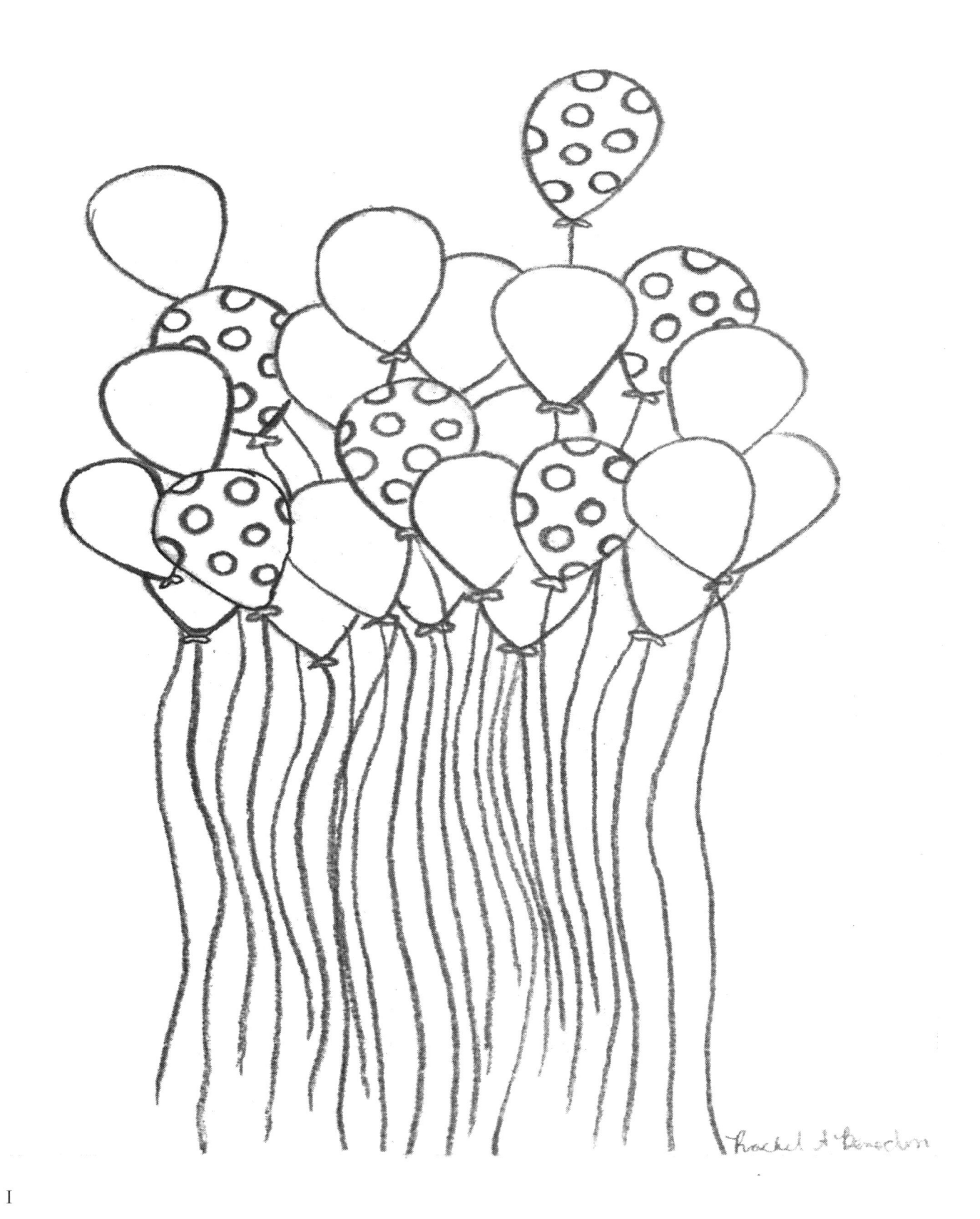

Being happy doesn't mean everything is perfect. It just means you've decided to look beyond the imperfections.
                                                            Gerard Way

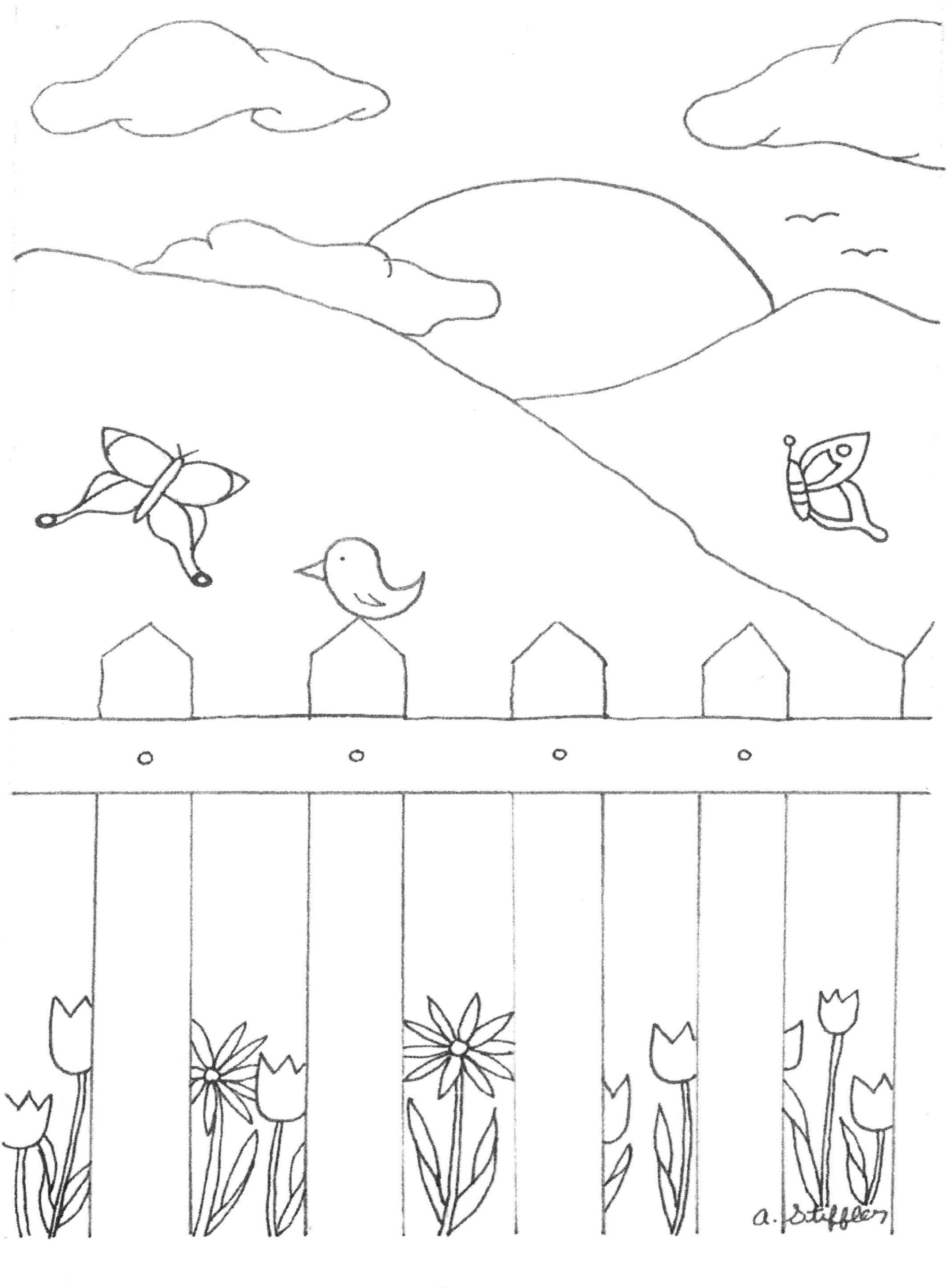
a. Stiffler

When you try to control everything, you enjoy nothing. Sometimes, you just need to relax, breathe, let go and live in the moment.
Author Unknown

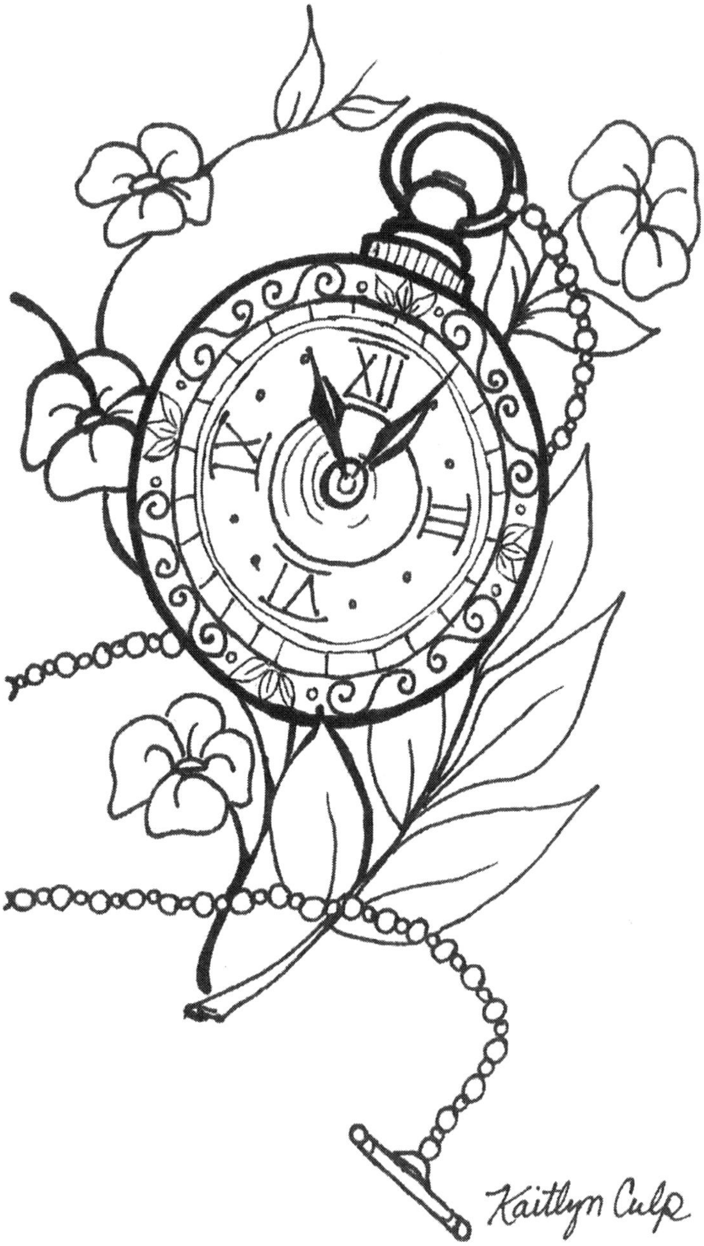
Kaitlyn Culp

The sun will rise and set regardless. What we choose to do with the light while it's here is up to us.

Alexandre Elle

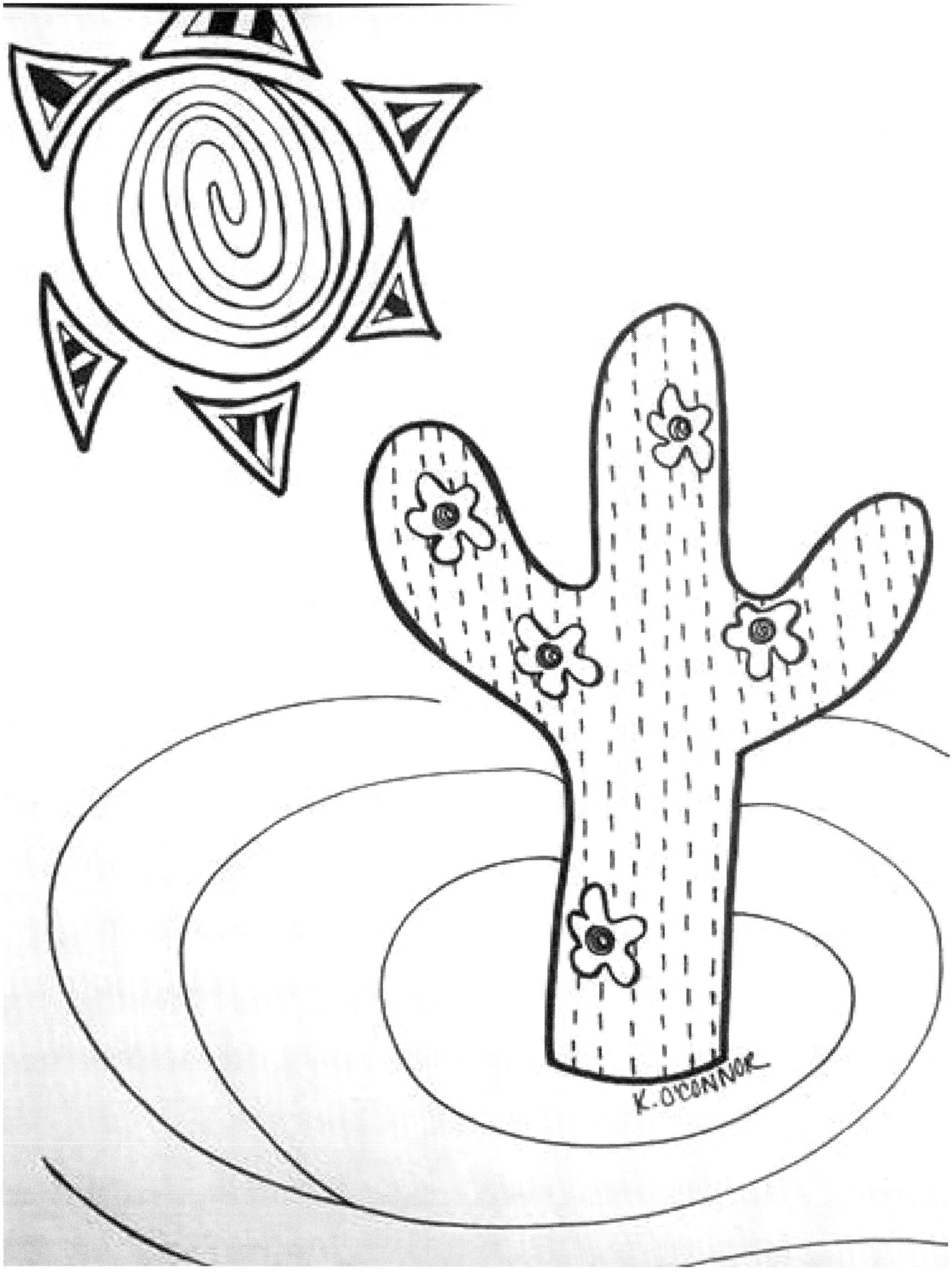
K. O'CONNOR

CHAPTER 7
ONGOING CONNECTIONS

It is often said that death ends a life, but not a relationship. As you color these pages, you can reflect on the ways that your loved one will continue to be a part of your life, and how you can keep your memories alive.

Love is how you stay alive, even after you are gone.
Mitch Albom

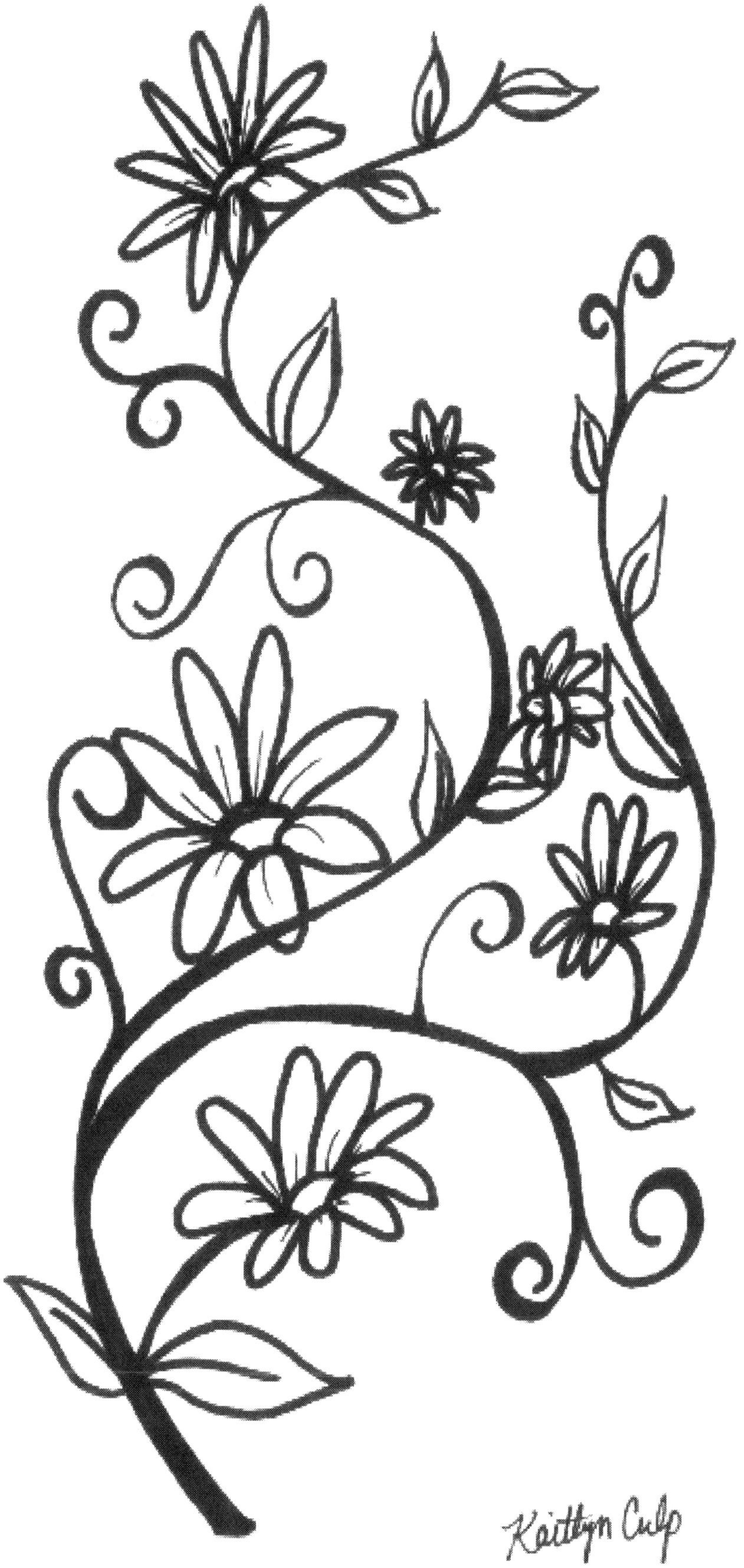

Kaitlyn Culp

Those whom we have loved never really leave us. They live on forever in our hearts, and cast their radiant light onto our every shadow.

Sylvana Rossetti

43

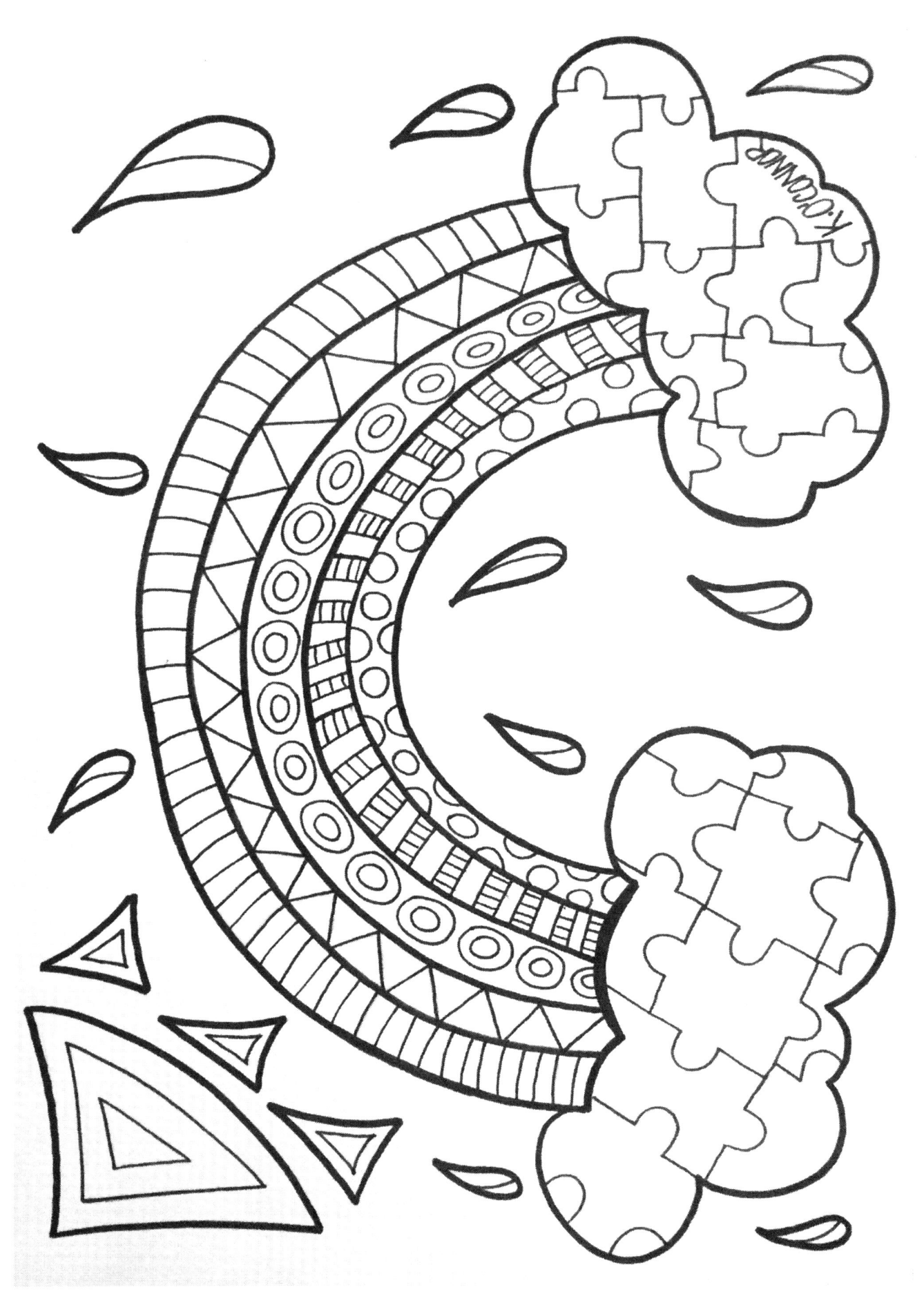

You are not forgotten loved one. Nor will you ever be. As long as life and memory last we will remember thee.
Author Unknown

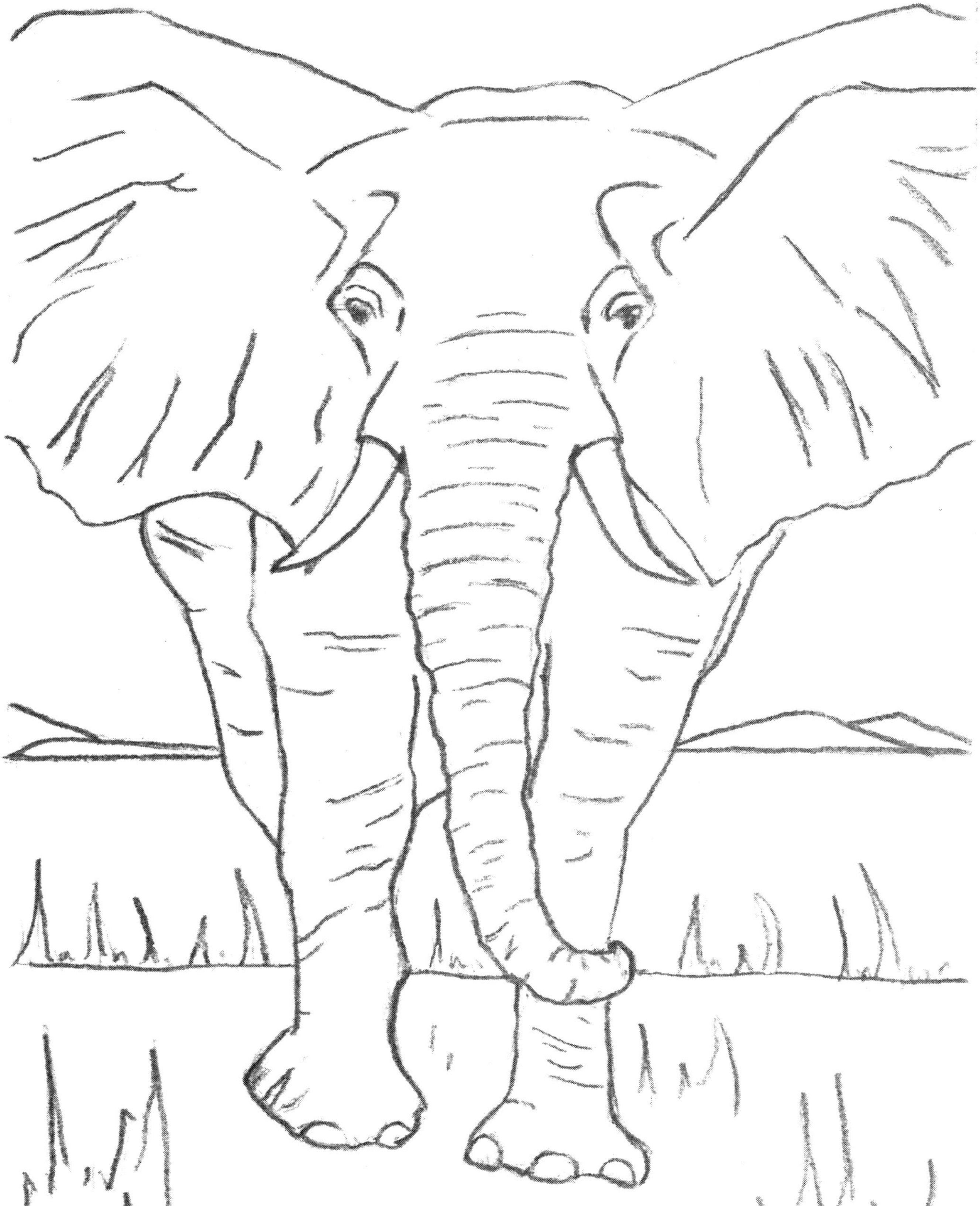

Like a bridge over troubled waters, I will ease your mind.
Paul Simon

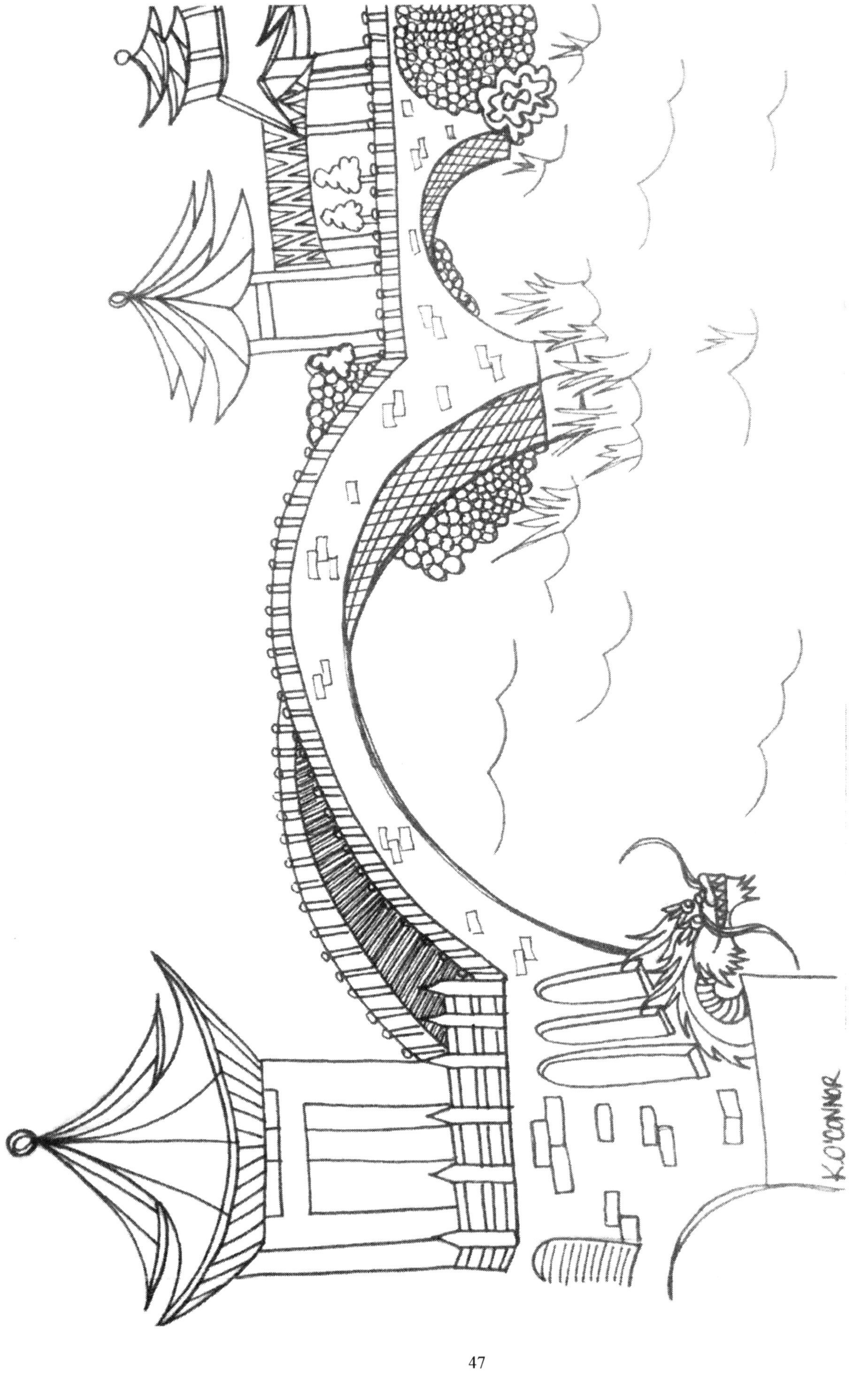
K.O'CONNOR

CHAPTER 8
REINVEST IN YOURSELF

As you continue to remember and be connected to your loved one, you can also be thinking about ways to reinvest in yourself. Take your time as you color the pictures in this section, allowing your mind to consider what it means for you to reinvest in yourself and re-engage with life.

Plan your hours to be productive. Plan your weeks to be educational. Plan your years to be purposeful. Plan your life to be an experience of growth. Plan to change. Plan to grow.
— *Iyanla Vanzant*

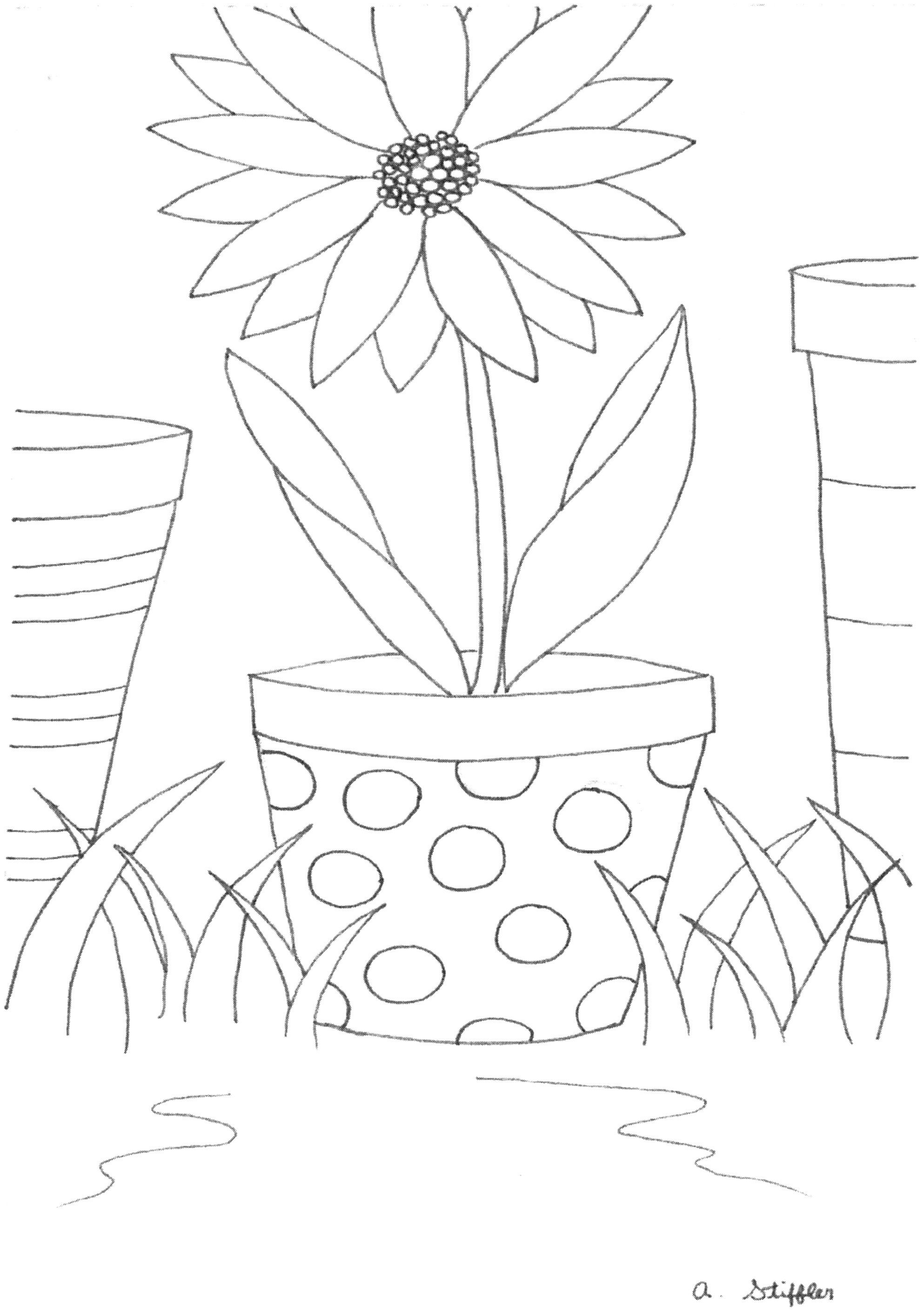
A. Stiffler

Hope is knowing that people, like kites, are made to be lifted up.
                                         Author Unknown

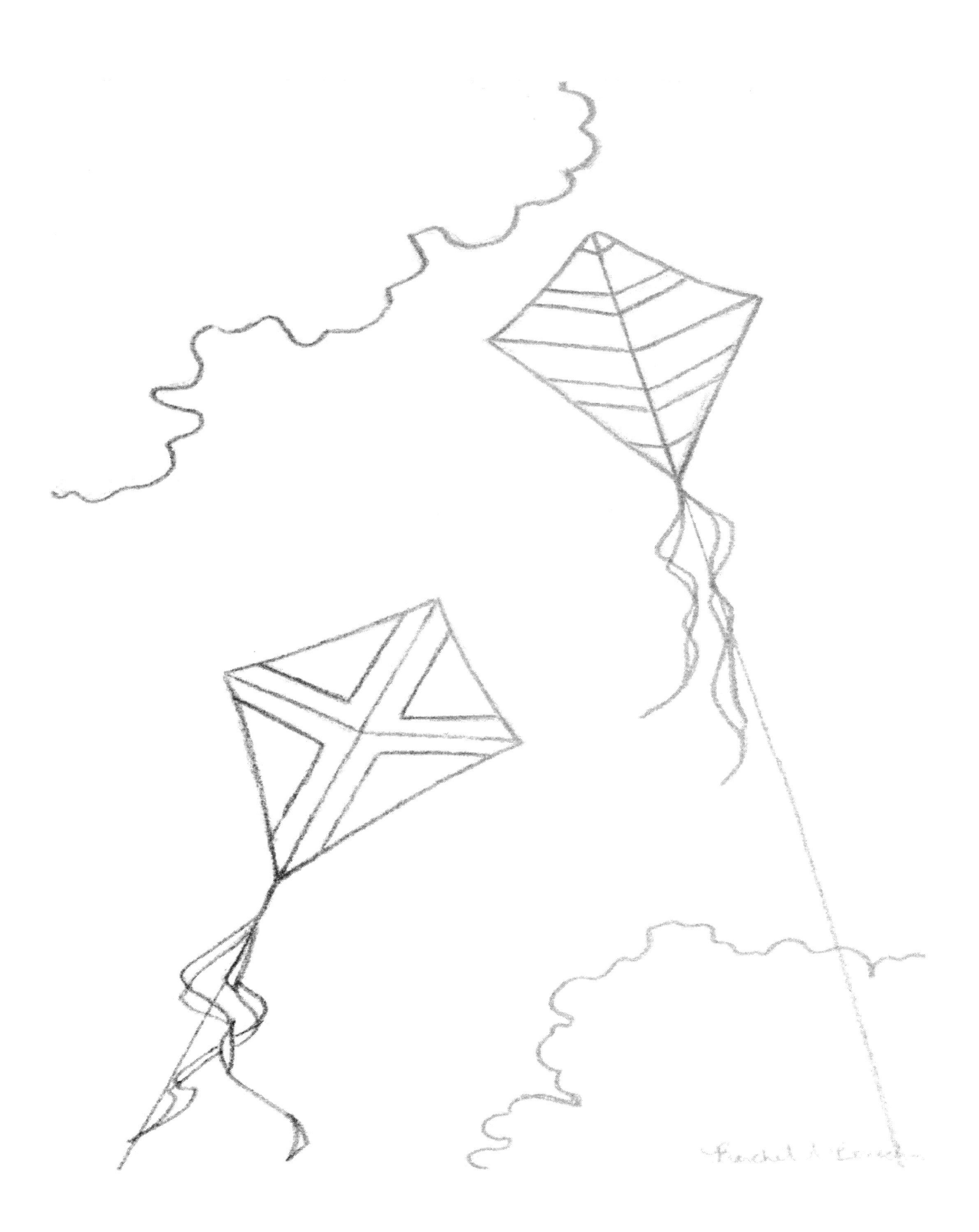

Today, find ways to reinvest in yourself – physically, spiritually, and emotionally.
Author Unknown

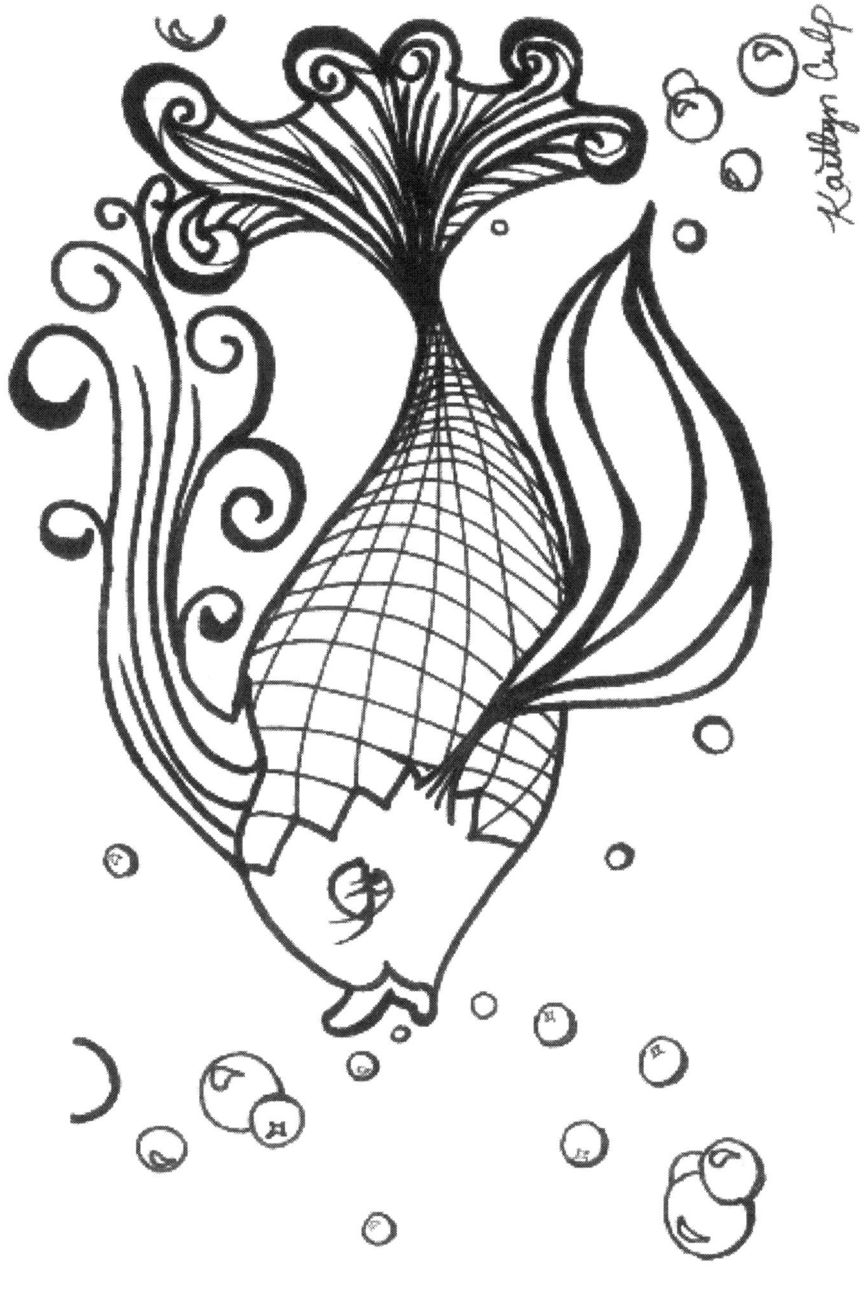
Kaitlyn Culp

And the time came when the risk to remain tight in a bud was more than the risk it took to blossom.
Anais Nin

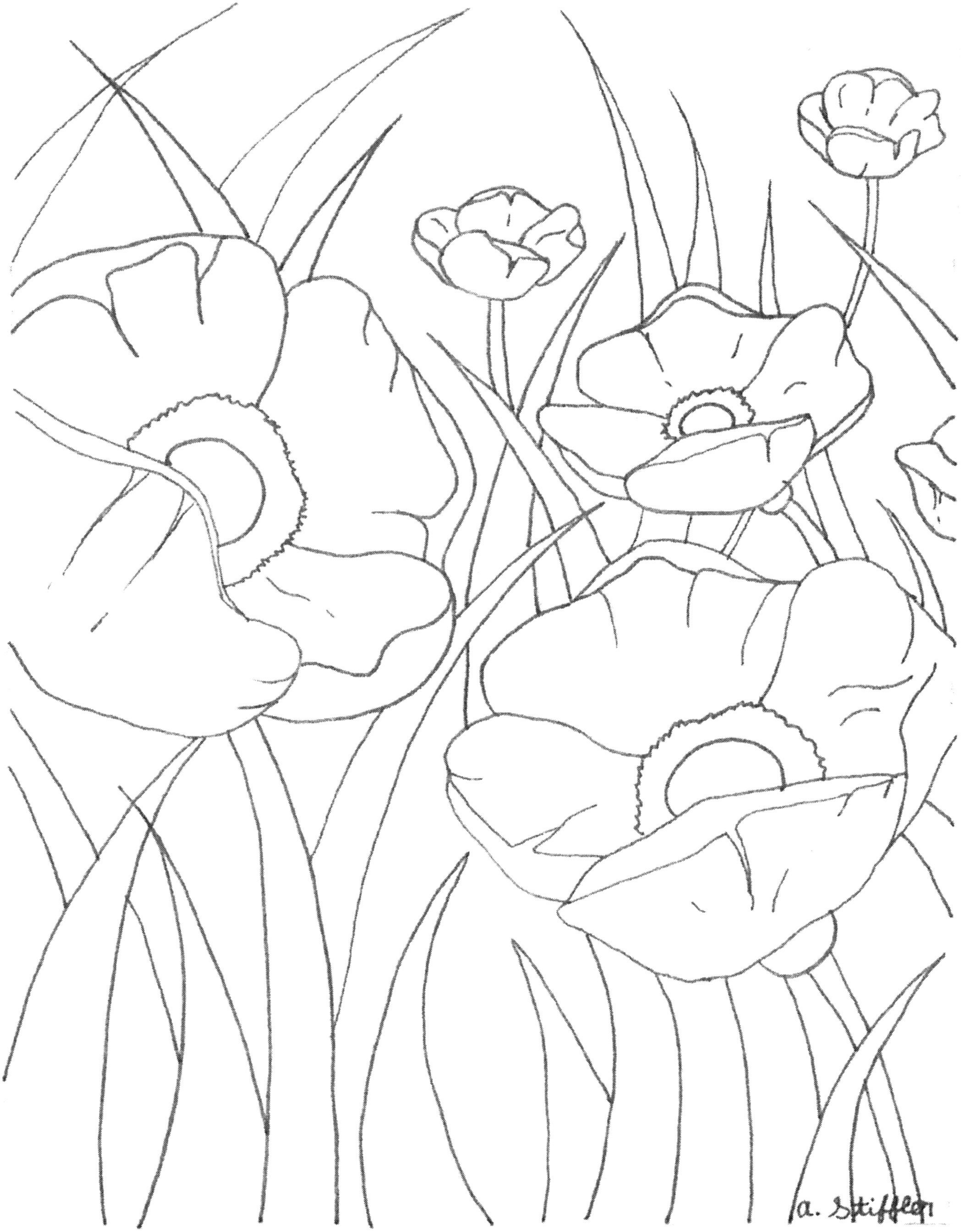
a. Stiffler

In the midst of winter, I found there was, within me, an invincible summer. And that makes me happy. For it says that no matter how hard the world pushes against me, within me, there's something stronger — something better, pushing right back.

— Albert Camus

59

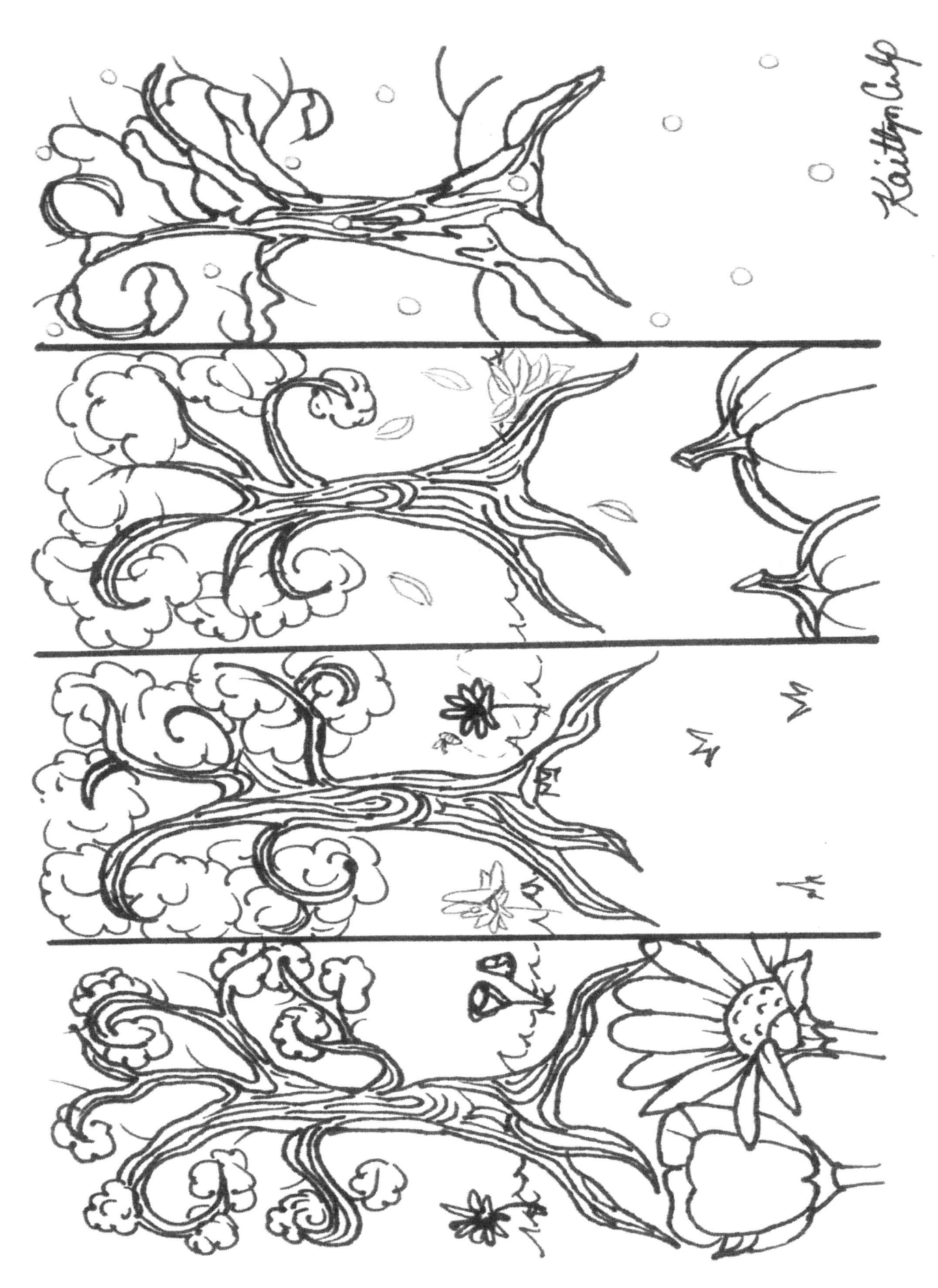

Made in the USA
San Bernardino, CA
18 March 2016